Turning Little Hearts

Over 90 Activities
to Connect Children with their Ancestors

by Jonah & Charlotte Barnes

CFI

An imprint of Cedar Fort, Inc.

Springville, Utah

This book is dedicated
to our six little children, of course!

ISBN 13: 978-1-4621-3694-0

Published by CFI, an imprint of Cedar Fort, Inc.
2373 W. 700 S., Springville, UT 84663
Distributed by Cedar Fort, Inc., www.cedarfort.com
Library of Congress Control Number: 2019952924

Cover and interior layout and design by Shawnda T. Craig
Cover design © 2019 Cedar Fort, Inc.
Edited by Heather Holm

Printed in the United States of America

10 9 8 7 6 5 4 3 2 1

Printed on acid-free paper

Contents

Tips for Using This Book

- These activities are best done with adults and children talking together. The adults share stories and information, and then the children do activities with them about what they just saw and heard.

- Most activities require a little preparation, such as learning a story about an ancestor beforehand or gathering craft supplies. But some can be done on the spot with no preparation.

- Some activity pages are just informational and do not need to be written on. But some activity pages have room for children to draw and write on. For those pages, it is nice to have additional copies of the book for multiple children. Or children can write on blank papers and keep them in a personal binder.

- Displaying old family photographs on frequently viewed walls will help keep the topic of ancestors on everyone's minds. Consider having a place to display the most recent activities your children did. This will help you and your children remember what was learned and felt.

- You decide how much overlap you want. You can do several activities about one ancestor. Or you can do one activity for each ancestor you have on record.

- These activities can be done with one child and one adult at the dinner table, many adults and many children at a family reunion, or any combination in between. Be flexible and creative!

- If you are struggling to think of old stories to tell, just start talking about your parents and grandparents. They are the grandparents and great-grandparents of your children, which is 3 and 4 generations back already. You don't have to look far for great stories.

- Remember, little hearts turn in little ways. Keep your activities short, simple, interesting, relatable, and fun. Do not force your children or bore them, and do not feel pressured to complete every line of every activity. Do as much as your children can happily handle in one sitting. Tasty treats at the end always help too.

Introduction

We wrote this book about your child. Yep, yours. This book is about them: their personality, their future, their life. It's all about them. It's only about them. In fact, this book is the most specific and personal book your child will ever read.

The trick is—this book isn't completed yet. There are nearly one hundred pages of games, activities; and crafts that need to be enjoyed. This book can only be finished with the help of you and your child. That's why it's the most intimate, impactful, and personal book they'll ever read.

In the 1990s, research in child development discovered some pretty amazing things about families. As thousands of diverse families were observed, scientists noticed a pattern: stable children know their history. Children who understand they are part of a larger picture—a chain of persons—gives them emotional stability, self-assurance, and happiness. They do better in school, get along better with their parents, and handle problems more easily. In fact, the researchers concluded that a strong family narrative was the single greatest predictor of emotional health and happiness.

How could this be? How could knowing a family narrative be a stronger benefit than, say, birth-order? IQ? Or socio-economic status?

Psychologists think the answer lies in the formation of memories. Memories are the building blocks of personality—even if a memory belongs to an ancestor. Children can draw on the experiences of their ancestors for a sense of self. If parents can make ancestral stories relevant to their child, these stories become the child's story.

Imagine being shoved onto a stage in the middle of a three-act play—better yet, a musical! The orchestra swells and the actors turn to you and the audience holds their breath, waiting for you to sing a solo. The trouble is, you have no idea what the script is, what the music is, or what your part is. How terrifying! This nightmare is what many teenagers experience as they are dropped onto the planet with no knowledge of where they came from. Friends, teachers, bosses, and driving instructors turn to them and await a performance—a solo. Our teenagers panic! They act out and rebel, of course. They don't know their story. They feel alone!

These children need to know their backstory. They need to know that their ancestors faced many of the same problems. Their grandmother dealt with her sisters. Their grandfather struggled in school. Their great-grandfather had to chase their great-grandmother. Their father had weird hair in high school. Their mother had weirder hair in high school!

If a child knows their family stories, they know how to better recover from mistakes, how to bear through problems, how to be patient, how to plan for the future. A child armed with their history might still get stage fright, but they can see their forefathers and foremothers behind the curtain off stage, cheering them on. "We did it! So can you!" Family stories give assurance, comfort, and confidence.

So, is this book really about your child's ancestors? No. It's about your child. *Turning Little Hearts* is about unlocking your child's story. Turning their heart to their ancestry will make them a happier child. (And maybe even make you a happier parent!) By the end of your journey through this book, we hope your child will learn more about themselves than from any other book.

See? We really did write this book about your child!

Do an Activity

See How Much You Know

You may call your grandparents by their nicknames, like "Gampa," "Nana," or "Granny-Great," but they all have real names. Do you know what they are? Try to fill in the family tree below by yourself with ancestors' names you know. Then ask your parents to help you fill in the remaining names. (This same activity is at the end of the book, so after you've finished all the activities, you can test yourself again. You will be amazed at your progress!)

MY FOUR-GENERATION FAMILY TREE

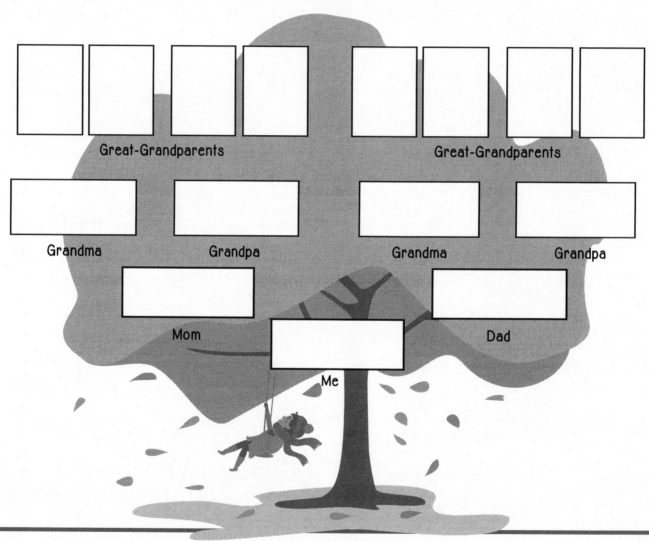

Great-Grandparents   Great-Grandparents

Grandma   Grandpa   Grandma   Grandpa

Mom   Dad

Me

How many of your ancestors' names did you know by yourself? _____

How many of your ancestors' names did your parents help you fill in? _____

How many of your ancestors' names did you and your parents have to look up? _____

Total ancestors in four-generation family tree: _____

BONUS: Can you write in some other distant ancestors' names that you know at the top of the tree?

Time Travel to an Ancestor

Imagine you found a time machine and traveled back in time to visit an ancestor. Perhaps you can build a time machine out of cardboard boxes or cushions and blankets in your house. Think about whom you would visit, what you would do, and what you would talk about.

Which ancestor would you visit?	When and where did they live?
What would you want to see in their town?	What would you like to do with him or her?
What questions would you like to ask?	How do you think he or she would respond?

Would you invite him or her to come back to your house in modern time?
What would you do together in your town?

Compare Trees and Families

Have you ever wondered why the image of a tree is so frequently used in connection with family history? Go outside and stand by a tree. Read about all the different parts of that tree. Then discuss how a tree is like a family.

PARTS OF A TREE

Leaves – Leaves absorb energy from the sun and change it into food (sugar) for the tree. They also soften the fall of rain, so it doesn't damage the important soil right around the tree.

Bark – Bark is like a suit of armor to protect the tree against the world. It protects the tree from sun, insects, storms, extreme temperatures, and disease.

Trunk – Strong trunks keep trees upright. Trunks also contain tubes that carry nutrients and water from the roots to the leaves, and they carry food (sugar) from the leaves to the roots.

Heartwood – You can't see the heartwood because it is the darker, older center of the trunk. Even though the heartwood is no longer alive, it provides great strength to the tree and is very resistant to decay.

Roots – You also won't be able to see roots, unless they are poking up above the ground. There are thousands of roots reaching out under the ground beneath each tree. They absorb water and nutrients from the soil, and they also keep the tree anchored to the ground. Without strong roots, a tree could easily fall over in a windstorm.

List three ways that our families and our ancestors are like the parts of a tree:

1. _____

2. _____

3. _____

Find Interesting Family Names

There are all sorts of names throughout history—funny names, difficult-to-pronounce names, foreign names, made-up names, named-after-famous-people names, and names with deep meaning. Look through your family tree and see if you can find the following kinds of names.

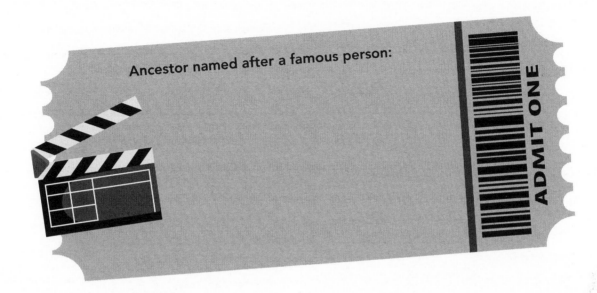

Ancestor named after a famous person:

ADMIT ONE

Most common name you found:

Ancestor who named a child after himself or herself:

BONUS

If you were to name one of your future children after an ancestor, what name would you choose?

_____

Why? _____

_____

_____

Research Your Namesake

A namesake is the person after whom you are named. Not everyone has one, but you might! Ask your parents if you have a namesake, and then take some time to learn about him or her. Use the blank face below to decorate your face and hair. Write your name underneath. Then answer the questions about your namesake.

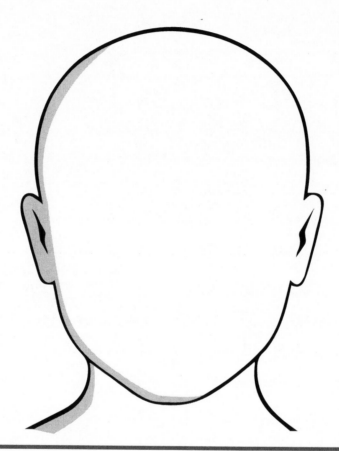

Who am I named after? _____

Why did my parents give me this name? _____
_____

Here are three facts about my namesake: _____
_____
_____
_____

What traits of my namesake do I share? _____

What other traits of my namesake would I like to emulate? _____
_____

Discover What You Are Made Of

You are not a random jumble of physical traits and personality traits. Actually, you are an assortment of traits all passed down from your ancestors! There isn't a new gene in your body! A little bit—or a lot—of each of your ancestors is in you. Draw yourself in the blank body and fill in whose traits you have.

Height is _____,
from _____.

Hair color is _____,
from _____.

Eye color is _____,
from _____.

My voice sounds _____,
just like _____.

My taste for food is _____,
just like _____.

My personality is _____,
similar to _____.

My talent for _____,
is from _____.

My love of _____,
is from _____.

My athletic ability for _____,
is from _____.

11

Fill In the Dash

On a gravestone, there are three common things: (1) a name, (2) a birthdate and a death date, and (3) a dash. The dash just separates the birthdate from the death date, but it also could represent everything that happened in that person's life. Think of that—everything they did was summed up in one big, blank dash. Give "the dash" of an ancestor meaning by researching some of his or her accomplishments and filling them in here. Fill out the headstone information too.

BIRTH DEATH
(   )-(   )

1. _____

2. _____

3. _____

4. _____

5. _____

6. _____

Make a Nationality Pie Chart

Even though you were born in one specific place, your body is made up of pieces from all over the world. This whole pie chart represents you. The slices represent your great-grandparents. Write one of their names in each section. Find out all the countries where they are from and assign a color to each country on the legend. Color the chart according to the countries each great-grandparent is from.

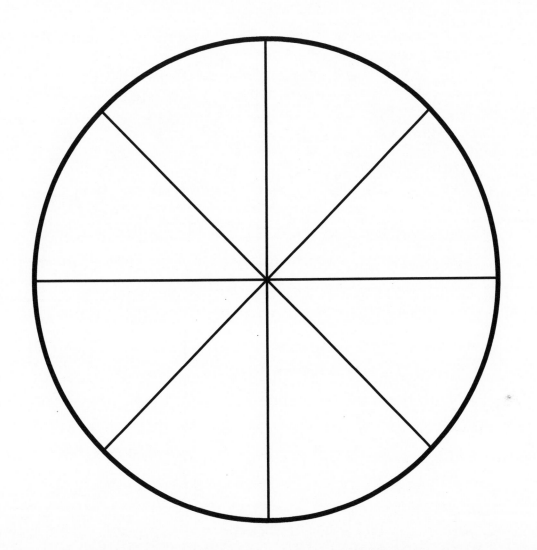

LEGEND			
☐ = _____		☐ = _____	
☐ = _____		☐ = _____	
☐ = _____		☐ = _____	
☐ = _____		☐ = _____	

Celebrate an Ancestor's Birthday

Even though most of your ancestors have passed away, you can still celebrate their birthdays. Chose whose birthday you will celebrate, plan the event, and then have the party.

Materials needed: various party supplies

Party Plan

DATE OF PARTY	LOCATION OF PARTY

PEOPLE TO INVITE	FOOD

GAMES	DECORATIONS	CAKE DÉCOR AND FLAVOR

ACTIVITY THAT THIS ANCESTOR LOVED	ACTIVITY TO HONOR THIS ANCESTOR

Learn Foreign Phrases

There is a high probability that your ancestors did not speak English. They likely spoke other languages, like Swedish, German, Spanish, or Russian. That's because they lived in far-off countries before they immigrated to America. Find out a language that an ancestor spoke and translate the following phrases into that language.

Materials needed: a foreign dictionary (book or online)

Hello. _____

My name is _____. _____

I live in _____. _____

I am ____ years old. _____

I'm hungry. _____

Where is the bathroom? _____

I love my family. _____

BONUS
Memorize these phrases and say them to a friend.

Learn an Ancestor's Skill

Many of your ancestors had unique trade skills they used to earn a living. They may have mined for coal, made pottery, crafted barrels, milked cows, braided rugs, ridden horses, herded sheep, or built rockets. Research one of those skills, and draw it here.

Ancestor's name: _____

Ancestor's skill: _____

_____

┌─────────────── BONUS ───────────────┐
Learn how to do this skill yourself, or find a place to see it in action.
Write your experience below
└──────────────────────────────────────┘

My experience: _____

_____

_____

Have an Old Clothing Fashion Show

Clothing trends change every few years depending on the needs, styles, and technology available. It's easy to look back at past generations and laugh at what they wore, but at the time, those clothes were in style and your ancestors loved them. Put on a fashion show of these old clothes.

Materials needed: old clothes, masking tape or rope, chairs

 DIRECTIONS

1. Gather old clothes from your parents' or grandparents' closets or some modern re-creations of old clothes.
2. Make space in your house for a runway and mark it with masking tape on the ground or with colorful rope.
3. Play some fun music and walk down the runway with your friends and family watching.

BONUS

Research what materials clothes in the 1800s were made from. How would it feel to wear that? What would daily work be like with those clothes? How many outfits and shoes did your long-ago ancestors have? How does that make you feel about the clothes that you have?

Celebrate Pioneers

Were any of your ancestors pioneers who left their old homes to find a new home? Maybe they sailed on a ship, maybe they rode in a wagon, or maybe they walked hundreds of miles to find a better place to live. It was probably a very long, difficult journey, but their sacrifice and determination bless you today.

List your pioneer ancestors, the years they moved, and one fact about their journeys.

ANCESTORS	YEARS	FACTS

Choose the ways you would like to celebrate your pioneer ancestors.

- Don't eat lunch, so you can feel hungry like many of the pioneers felt
- Draw a picture of a pioneer ancestor and hang it in your house
- Make butter by shaking whipping cream in a glass jar
- Tell a friend about a pioneer ancestor
- Watch a movie about pioneers
- Bake your own bread
- Ride a horse
- Cook your dinner over a fire
- Watch a movie about pioneers
- Walk barefoot outside for a while
- Share stories of pioneer ancestors
- Reenact a mini pioneer trek near your house
- Sing pioneer songs at home or on top of a mountain
- Make covered wagon models out of various snacks and candy

DO AN ACTIVITY

Celebrate Resurrection on Easter

Easter is the day that we celebrate when Jesus Christ overcame death and was resurrected. Without Him, we would all be dead and alone forever. But because of Him, we will all live again, and we can be with our families *and our ancestors* forever! In the midst of the Easter egg hunts and bunny rabbits, take some time to remember and celebrate the true meaning of Easter.

Visit a cemetery where an ancestor is buried, or any local cemetery, and read John 20.

Do you have an ancestor who was injured or disabled, who will have a perfect body one day?

Make a Christ-themed Easter egg hunt. (See below)

Discuss what will happen to bodies at the resurrection.

Discuss how Jesus Christ gave hope to everyone who has had a family member die.

Build a model of the empty tomb out of clay or nature items you find outside. Display the empty tomb.

Make Resurrection Rolls. (See below)

Talk about a deceased ancestor you are excited to meet one day. What will you ask him or her?

RESURRECTION ROLLS

1. Unroll a package of prepared crescent roll dough.
2. Sprinkle cinnamon and sugar on the dough triangles.
3. Place a marshmallow on each triangle.
4. Wrap the dough around the marshmallow, pinching all sides to completely cover the marshmallow.
5. Bake the rolls at 375° for 12 min.
6. When you bite into the rolls, the bread is empty—just like Jesus's tomb.

CHRIST-THEMED EASTER EGG HUNT

Among your candy-filled eggs, place ten numbered eggs with the following items inside. Instruct kids to collect them, but don't open them until everyone is gathered together at the end and can discuss the contents of the special eggs.

1. Sacrament bread (to symbolize the Last Supper)
2. Sacrament water cup (to also symbolize the Last Supper)
3. Red paper in drop shape (to symbolize Christ bleeding in Gethsemane)
4. Rope (to symbolize Jesus being tied up)
5. Soap (to symbolize Pilate washing his hands clean after condemning Jesus to death)
6. Thorn (to symbolize the crown of thorns)
7. Dice (to symbolize the soldiers casting lots for Christ's clothes)
8. Wooden cross (to symbolize Jesus's cross)
9. White cloth folded (to symbolize the linens Jesus's body was wrapped in)
10. Empty (to symbolize the empty tomb)

Tell a Family Story at Dinner

During family dinnertime, we strengthen our bodies *and* we strengthen our families. Scientists have found that when a family sits and eats dinner together, the kids are smarter, happier, and better prepared to resist bad things. Telling family stories during dinner is an excellent way to further strengthen you and your family at dinner.

Draw your favorite dinner here:

Here are some questions about my ancestors that I want to ask at dinnertime:

1. _____

2. _____

3. _____

Here are some family history stories I want to share at dinnertime:

1. _____

2. _____

3. _____

Make a Favorite Family Recipe

Food traditions run deeply in all families. Your grandfather may have a sweet tooth produced by his mother's oatmeal raisin cookies. Your grandmother may have a secret recipe for rolls that she made for every family holiday dinner. Ask an ancestor for a favorite family recipe and write it here.

Materials needed: old family favorite recipe

Bonus materials needed: cooking supplies and ingredients

RECIPE .... SERVES ....

FROM THE KITCHEN OF .... **PREP TIME** ....

INGREDIENTS

....

....

....

....

....

....

DIRECTIONS

....

....

....

....

....

....

BONUS

BONUS #1: Make the recipe.

BONUS #2: Write about a time this food was made and enjoyed in the past.

BONUS #3: Write your favorite recipe that you want to pass down to your children.

Host a Cultural Celebration

Your ancestors who lived in distant countries celebrated different holidays than the ones you are used to. They had unique traditions of food, clothing, music, and dancing. Choose a foreign holiday from your family history, plan how to celebrate it, and then do it!

Materials needed: desired celebration supplies, decorations, clothing, music, and food

Ancestor's name: _____

Name of holiday: _____

Reason for celebrating: _____

_____

	WHAT ANCESTOR DID	WHAT I WILL DO
Date		
Food		
Decorations		
Music		
Clothing		
Ceremony or Activities		

BONUS

What was your favorite part of the holiday?
Why do you think this holiday was special for your ancestor?

Put On a Play

Think of a story in your family's history that you would like to produce on stage. Write a script for the actors with notes about what they should be doing while speaking. Gather some costumes and set up an area to perform. Then ask your friends and family to come watch you.

Materials needed: whatever props and costumes your play calls for

Here is my plan for the play:

Ancestor's name: _____

Story: _____

_____

_____

_____

_____

Actors: _____

_____

Audience: _____

_____

Place of performance: _____

Date of performance: _____

Additional notes: _____

_____

_____

_____

Plant a Garden

Your grandmothers and great-grandmothers all had favorite flowers. Perhaps they planted their favorite flowers around their houses, or perhaps they enjoyed buying a bouquet from the store. Find out some of their favorite flowers and draw those on the stems in this picture.

Materials needed: crayons

Bonus materials needed: seeds of your ancestors' favorite flowers, craft sticks, laminated copies of photographs of your ancestors

BONUS

Buy seeds of your ancestors' favorite flowers and plant them at your house. Then label them by making little craft stick signs with each grandmother's name and the flower's name.

Discuss the "Do You Know?" Test

This is a test written by a scientist named Robin Fivush. She found that kids who know more of their family stories have higher self-esteem, higher academic competence, higher social competence, and fewer behavioral problems ("The 'Do You Know?' 20 Questions about Family Stories," *Psychology Today*, Nov. 19, 2016). Take this test to see how well you know your family stories. Discuss the answers you know and don't know with your parents or grandparents. After you find all the answers, enjoy greater academic and social success in the years to come!

• • • DO YOU KNOW? • • •

1. Do you know how your parents met?
2. Do you know where your mother grew up?
3. Do you know where your father grew up?
4. Do you know where some of your grandparents grew up?
5. Do you know where some of your grandparents met?
6. Do you know where your parents were married?
7. Do you know what went on when you were being born?
8. Do you know the source of your name?
9. Do you know some things about what happened when your brothers or sisters were being born?
10. Do you know which person in your family you look most like?
11. Do you know which person in your family you act most like?
12. Do you know some of the illnesses and injuries that your parents experienced when they were younger?
13. Do you know some of the lessons that your parents learned from good or bad experiences?
14. Do you know some things that happened to your mom or dad when they were in school?
15. Do you know the national background of your family (such as English, German, Russian, etc.)?
16. Do you know some of the jobs that your parents had when they were young?
17. Do you know some awards that your parents received when they were young?
18. Do you know the names of the schools that your mom went to?
19. Do you know the names of the schools that your dad went to?
20. Do you know about a relative whose face "froze" in a grumpy position because he or she did not smile enough?

https://www.psychologytoday.com/us/blog/the-stories-our-lives/201611/the-do-you-know-20-questions-about-family-stories

Make Gravestone Rubbings

When your ancestors died, their bodies were buried in a cemetery. A headstone over each ancestor's grave lists his or her name, birthday, death day, and other details. Sometimes beautiful borders or pictures are added too. Visit your deceased ancestor's grave and make a rubbing of their headstone. Place a large piece of paper over the headstone to cover it. Take your unwrapped crayon, turn it on its side, and rub it over the paper. As you do that, the carvings under the paper will appear!

Materials needed: headstone, large paper, crayons with paper removed

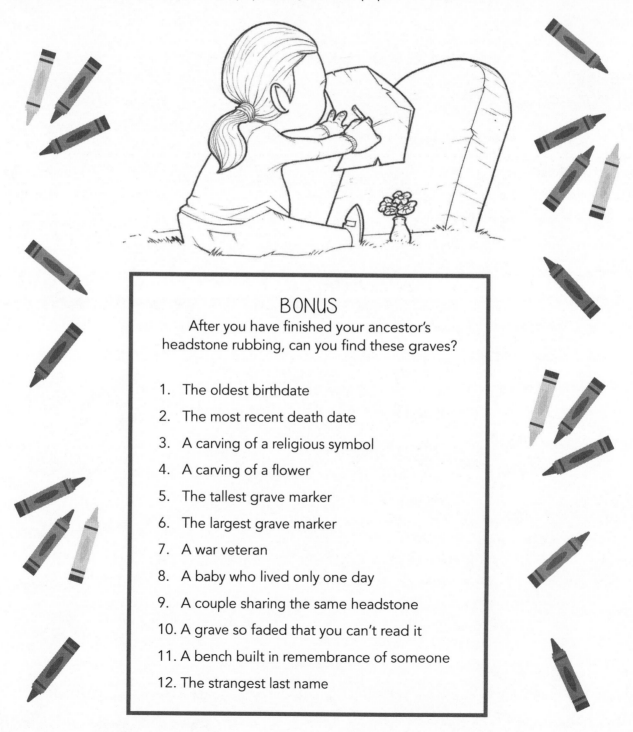

BONUS
After you have finished your ancestor's
headstone rubbing, can you find these graves?

1. The oldest birthdate

2. The most recent death date

3. A carving of a religious symbol

4. A carving of a flower

5. The tallest grave marker

6. The largest grave marker

7. A war veteran

8. A baby who lived only one day

9. A couple sharing the same headstone

10. A grave so faded that you can't read it

11. A bench built in remembrance of someone

12. The strangest last name

Visit a Place Your Ancestors Went

We can connect with our ancestors as we visit places that meant something to them. Plan a trip to an old house they lived in, a school they attended, a business where they worked, a mountain they climbed, a place they visited, a building they loved, a church they attended, a street they wandered, a park they played in, or an ice cream shop they loved. If the original structure no longer exists, go there anyway and learn about what used to be there.

If you can't easily travel to a place across the country or the world, use Google Maps to digitally explore. You'll be surprised at all the places those camera cars have been!

Write about your visit here: _____

_____

_____

_____

_____

_____

Use No Electricity for a Day

Before 1900, no one had electricity at home. Before 1930, no one had refrigerators or furnaces. Your great-grandparents and everyone before them lived a life without light bulbs, refrigerators, heaters, microwaves, ovens, phones, TVs, instant hot water, or cars. Can you live without those things for a day?

This is my plan for surviving a day without electricity:

How I will eat:_____

_____

How I will keep my body at a comfortable temperature: _____

_____

How I will see in the dark: _____

How I will entertain myself: _____

_____

How I will do my chores: _____

_____

How I will travel around: _____

This was my experience living without electricity: _____

_____

_____

_____

Make a Family Word Tree

What words come to your mind when you think of your family? Do you think about names? Do you think about places or accomplishments or character traits? Do you think about your own feelings? Put all these words together on a Family Word Tree.

Materials needed: poster board, brown marker, green construction paper, glue, scissors, pens

 DIRECTIONS

1. Draw a tree trunk with bare branches on a poster board.
2. Cut out a pile of leaves from the green construction paper.
3. On each leaf, write a word that describes your family—anyone from yourself to your siblings to your great-grandparents.
4. Glue the leaves to the bare branches on the poster.
5. Hang it up for anyone to see and for other family members to make additional leaves.

Tell a Family Bedtime Story

Do you have a favorite book to read at bedtime or a favorite story to hear? Bedtime stories help us relax before falling asleep. Ask your parents to tell you a story tonight. Maybe the story can be about a crazy place they or an ancestor slept. Tomorrow morning, write about the story here.

BONUS
Create a real book of your own with this story. Make several pages with illustrations and a cover. Then read your book to a family member at bedtime.

Share a Family Story during Family Night

All families can benefit from a Family Home Evening—a special time set aside during each week to learn together, play together, and enjoy a treat together. Consider doing this with your family. For one of your special evenings, share a story and a picture about an ancestor. Perhaps it can be about how an ancestor's family grew stronger together. After you share the story, ask your family members questions to make sure they were listening!

This week I am going to share this story and this picture.

Go on a Treasure Hunt

Following scavenger hunt clues or an old-looking treasure map to find a surprise is a great adventure. Hide an ancestor-themed treasure (along with some candy!) in your house or yard. Either make a map to guide others to the item, or write and hide a series of clues leading from one place in your house to the next. When the surprise is found, eat the candy and tell everyone how this ancestor item is like a special treasure.

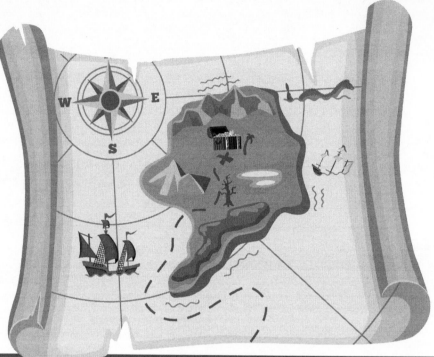

BONUS
Share a story about an ancestor finding something of great worth.
Did they find wealth through a great job? Did they ever win a prize or an award?
Did they ever reach a lofty goal or dream? Did they find something they lost?
Did they find a sibling who was lost?

Write the story here:

Cause and Effect

Whether or not your ancestors knew it, many of the choices they made affected you! From where they chose to live, to what job they had, from what church they attended, to what causes they chose to fight for. Find out a choice your ancestor made and ponder how it affected you.

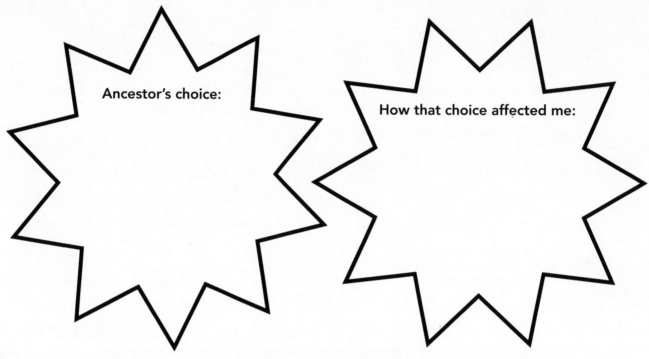

Ancestor's choice:

How that choice affected me:

BONUS
Now think about a choice you can make
and how it will affect your future family.

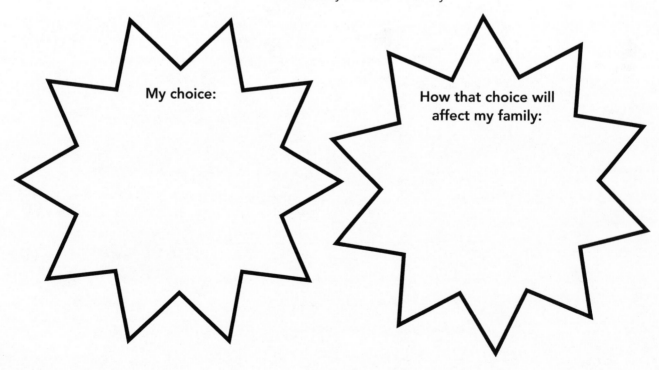

My choice:

How that choice will
affect my family:

Childhood Chores

What chores are you responsible for doing? Taking out the trash, cleaning your room, or mowing the lawn? Your ancestors probably had a lot more chores than that. Some woke up before the sun rose and worked on farms all day, all year long. Learn about their chores and record them here.

Ancestor's name: _____

Ancestor's birthyear: _____

Where he or she grew up: _____

Chores he or she did: _____

_____

_____

_____

In your opinion, which chore was the hardest? Why? _____

_____

_____

_____

BONUS
Find a way to act out or actually do the chores your ancestor did.

Education

Getting a good education can open minds, open doors, and improve lives greatly. Some of your ancestors sacrificed a lot to obtain basic schooling. Some became the first in their families to go to college. Find an ancestor who worked hard to get an education and write about him or her.

Ancestor's name: _____

Where and when did he or she attend school? _____

_____

How did he or she get to school? _____

What did he or she study? _____

_____

_____

How did education help him or her in life? _____

_____

_____

_____

BONUS
Do an activity to recreate your ancestor's school experience. (Walk the distance that they walked to school, practice using a small chalkboard and chalk, learn about a topic they studied, etc.)

Common Foods

Your ancestors ate food that was very different from what you eat today. Chicken nuggets and fruit snacks weren't even around! Research a food that an ancestor would have eaten, eat it, and write about your experience.

Ancestor's name: _____

Where he or she lived: _____

Strange food he or she ate: _____

Where can I buy this, or how can I make this? _____

_____

_____

This food tasted like: _____

I want to eat this food again (check one) ☐ YES ☐ NO

This is a picture of me eating it.

Animals and Pets

Pets make great companions and can be great helpers too. Nowadays, we frequently have dogs, cats, or fish. But your ancestors likely had sheep, pigs, horses, cows, donkeys, or chickens. Find out what animal or pet one of your ancestors had and write about it.

Ancestor's name: _____

Animal type: _____

Animal name: _____

Purpose of this animal: _____

_____

Memories your ancestor has of this animal: _____

_____

_____

_____

_____

_____

Photo or drawing of ancestor's animal:

BONUS
Find one of these animals in your community and visit it. Talk with the owner and learn more about taking care of this animal.

Sports

Sports are a great way to have fun, make friends, get fit, learn teamwork, and experience winning and losing. What sports do you play? What sports did your ancestors play? Write about one of those sports here, and answer the questions.

Ancestor's name: _____

Sport played: _____

Where did he or she play this sport? _____

On what team did he or she play? _____

Did he or she get any injuries while playing? _____

Go out and play this sport. If that's not possible, try playing a simplified version at home with your family. Write about your experience playing this sport.

_____

_____

_____

This is a drawing of my ancestor doing this sport.

BONUS
Find a picture of your ancestor playing this sport and display it in your house next to a picture of you playing this sport.

Music

Do you have a musical ancestor? See if you can listen to and sing the songs they sang. If your ancestor played an instrument, track down that instrument and watch someone play it, or see if you can play it yourself. Draw a picture of your musical ancestor below.

Ancestor's name: _____

Instrument played: _____

Story about this ancestor and music: _____

_____

_____

_____

_____

Wedding Photographs

No matter where in the world or when in history, weddings have always been special events. People gather from far and wide to celebrate the beginning of the bride and groom's new life together. Find a few photographs of your ancestors on their wedding days. (This can include your own parents!) Put the photos side by side and answer these questions, and then paste or draw the pictures below.

1. **How do the brides' dresses and grooms' suits compare?** _____

   _____

2. **What do you observe about the bridesmaids or groomsmen?** _____

   _____

3. **What kinds of flowers are the brides holding?** _____

   _____

4. **How did the couples meet?** _____

   _____

5. **What are stories about their wedding day?** _____

   _____

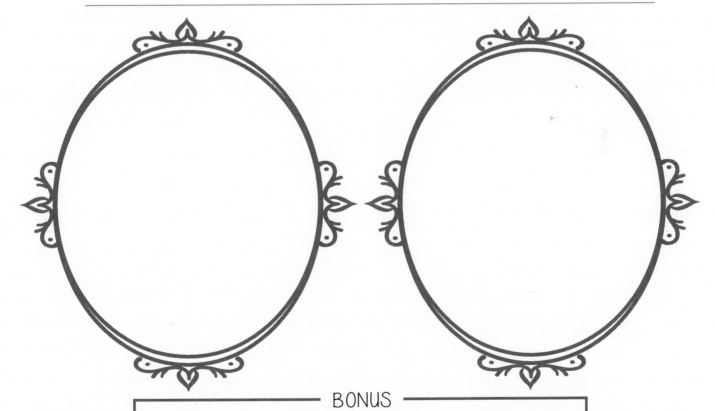

=== BONUS ===
Put your ancestors' wedding photographs in a collage frame or in several frames next to each other and display them in your house.

Businesses and Jobs

What jobs did your ancestors have? Some may have owned their own businesses, others may have jumped from job to job each year, and others may have had the same job their whole lives. Research a job that an ancestor had and write about it here.

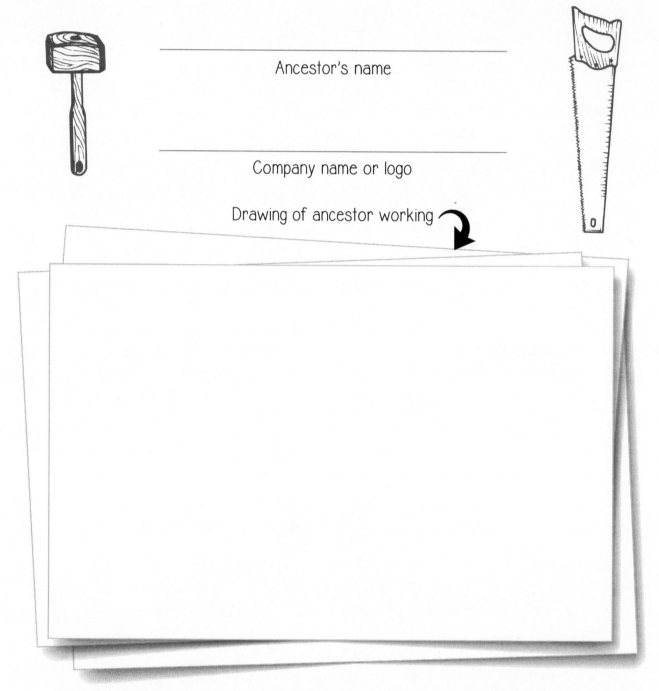

_____

Ancestor's name

_____

Company name or logo

Drawing of ancestor working

BONUS
With your family, do a hands-on and fun activity to re-create a task they did at work. (Toss newspapers on porches, type on an old typewriter, pretend to be a nurse, etc.)

Religious Convert

Somewhere in your family tree are ancestors who grew up practicing one religion but then converted to a different religion. Write about one of those ancestors here.

Ancestor's name: _____

Hometown: _____

Previous religion: _____

New religion: _____

Year of conversion: _____

Testimony: _____

_____

_____

_____

_____

_____

_____

_____

BONUS
Can you identify all the religious converts in your family tree?
Make a family tree on a separate paper and highlight them all.

Outdoor Survivor

A few generations ago, your family members had no electricity, running water, heaters, microwaves, chainsaws, canned food, or grocery stores. They grew their own food, hauled water from streams, and chopped wood for fires. Each of them was so resourceful and strong! Imagine you traveled back in time and were stuck in a huge forest. Which of your tough ancestors would you choose to bring with you? Write about it here.

My ancestor's name: _____

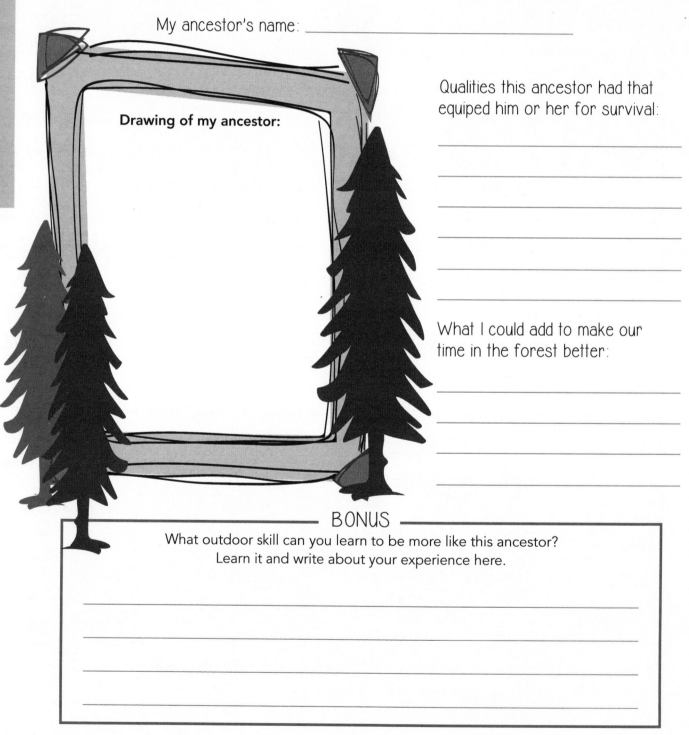

Drawing of my ancestor:

Qualities this ancestor had that equiped him or her for survival:

_____
_____
_____
_____
_____
_____

What I could add to make our time in the forest better:

_____
_____
_____
_____

BONUS

What outdoor skill can you learn to be more like this ancestor?
Learn it and write about your experience here.

_____
_____
_____
_____

Wartime Experience

Did any of your ancestors serve in a war as a soldier, a pilot, a doctor, an engineer, or something else? They certainly were brave heroes. If you don't have an ancestor who served in a war, you most likely have an ancestor whose life was affected by war. Wars of all kinds can change how and where people live. Learn about the wartime experience of an ancestor and record it here.

Ancestor's name: _____

War name and dates: _____

_____

Where he or she served or lived: _____

_____

Wartime story: _____

_____

_____

_____

_____

_____

How was his or her life affected by the war? _____

_____

_____

_____

_____

_____

_____

_____

— BONUS —

Find objects such as medals, uniforms, or ration cards from that ancestor's time in war.
Can you re-create an experience such as boot camp, toy gun target practice, or blackouts?

Journal Entry

Some of your ancestors kept journals. Perhaps they wrote about the things they liked, the things they did, their accomplishments, or their trials. It's insightful to read about their lives from their own perspectives. Find an old journal that an ancestor kept and write about it here.

My ancestor's name: _____

Date of journal entry: _____

Ancestor's age: _____

**Copy the journal entry here, draw what it was about,
or summarize it in your own words.**

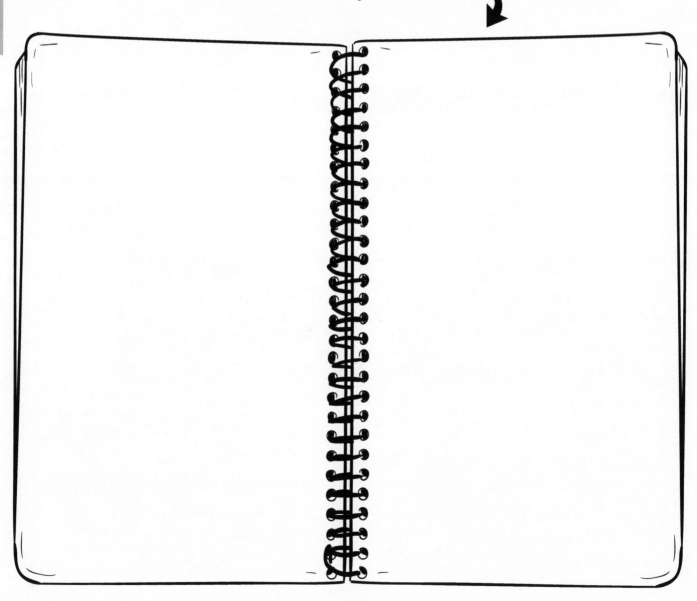

Poem

Some of your ancestors may have written poems. Poems are powerful and beautiful ways to share deep feelings. Some poems rhyme, some are silly, and some even make people cry. Find a poem that one of your ancestors wrote and write it here.

── BONUS ──

BONUS #1:
Memorize your ancestor's poem.

BONUS #2:
Write a poem for your future children. It can be about your family, or it can be about anything else.

Personal Motto

Throughout their lives, your ancestors learned important lessons that helped them live better, work harder, and love more deeply. Often, these lessons could be summed up in a short phrase called a motto. Find out an ancestor's motto and write it here.

Ancestor's motto:

What can you learn from this motto?

BONUS #1
Create a nice design with an ancestor's motto that you can display in your room.

BONUS #2
Write your own motto to live by.

Illness and Injury

When people get hurt or sick, their lives can change dramatically. Sometimes they experience miraculous recoveries, but other times they must adjust to a new way of moving and living. Learn about an ancestor whose life was affected by an illness or an injury. Then write about it and draw him or her in the space below.

Ancestor's name: _____

Injury and date he or she was injured: _____

_____

Did he or she recover? _____

_____

How did this affect his or her life afterward? _____

_____

_____

_____

_____

_____

─── BONUS ───
Make an activity to help you experience how your ancestor had to adjust after his or her injury. (Use crutches, try to hear with noise-canceling headphones on, cook with only one hand, etc.)

Handmade Item

Do you have any creative ancestors who painted, carved, built, knit, wove, or sewed? If they had that skill, maybe you have that skill too! Find something your ancestor made, or ask to hear a story about it. Then fill out this sheet.

Materials needed: handmade item from ancestor (or story about one)

Bonus materials needed: craft supplies to copy your ancestor's handmade item.

Ancestor's name:

_____

Item he or she made:

_____

_____

Drawing or photo of item:

What is the item made of? _____

How was the item made? _____

_____

How long do you think it took to make? _____

What purpose did the item have? _____

_____

_____

BONUS
Can you make something like this?
If you can, do it, and then write about it here.

_____

_____

_____

Heirloom

An heirloom is a valuable object that has been in a family for generations. Find an heirloom in your house that an ancestor once had in his or her house. Perhaps it's a pot, a stool, a painting, a purse, a cane, or a book. Learn about it, and then draw a picture of it and record what you learned here.

Ancestor's name:

_____

Heirloom:

_____

_____

What meaning or purpose did this object have to your ancestor? _____

_____

_____

What meaning does it have to you? _____

_____

_____

This is a picture of my ancestor's heirloom.

Birthplace Map

{ I was born in _____ , on this day _____ .

This is an interesting fact about my birth: _____
_____ }

You have ancestors who were born in countries all over the world. It's neat to see where everyone came from and how that led to your location today. Use the blank map on the following page to mark where some of your ancestors were born. Draw their faces and write their names in the boxes on the top and bottom, and then draw a line to the place where each ancestor was born.

Materials needed: the map on the next page

Bonus materials needed: large wall map, photos of your ancestors' faces, string, sewing pins

— BONUS —
Make a bigger, more permanent birthplace map to display in your home. Find a large world map to hang on your wall. Print photographs of the ancestors you want to include. Glue their pictures to the sides of the map, and then use a pin to attach a string and connect it from an ancestor's photo to a pin on his or her birthplace. Or make little flags with an ancestor's face or name on each of the pins and stick a flagged pin on each birthplace.

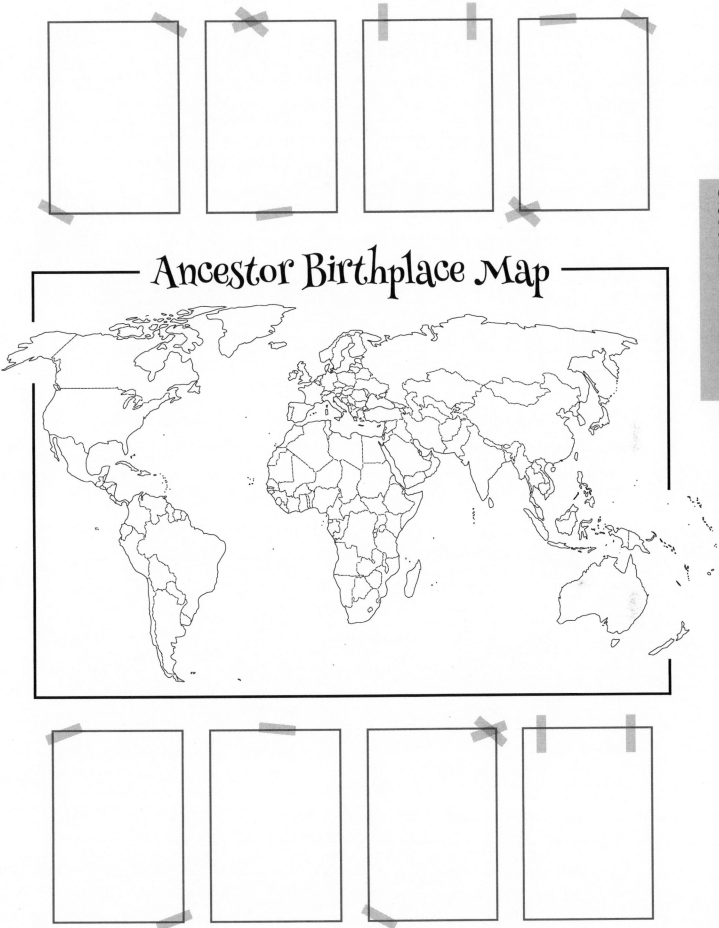

Ancestor Birthplace Map

Immigration Map

Many of your ancestors were born in one country, but then, for various reasons, moved to a different country. Fill out the information below for one ancestor and his or her immigration experience. Then use the map on the following page to trace the immigration routes of all your immigrant ancestors. Put their faces and names in the boxes, and then draw lines to their routes.

Materials needed: the map on the next page

Ancestor's name: _____

Date of immigration: _____

Why did he or she leave? _____

Where did the journey begin? _____

Where did they stop along the way? _____

_____

Where did the journey end? _____

What is a story from their journey? _____

_____

Story: _____

_____

_____

_____

_____

_____

_____

_____

_____

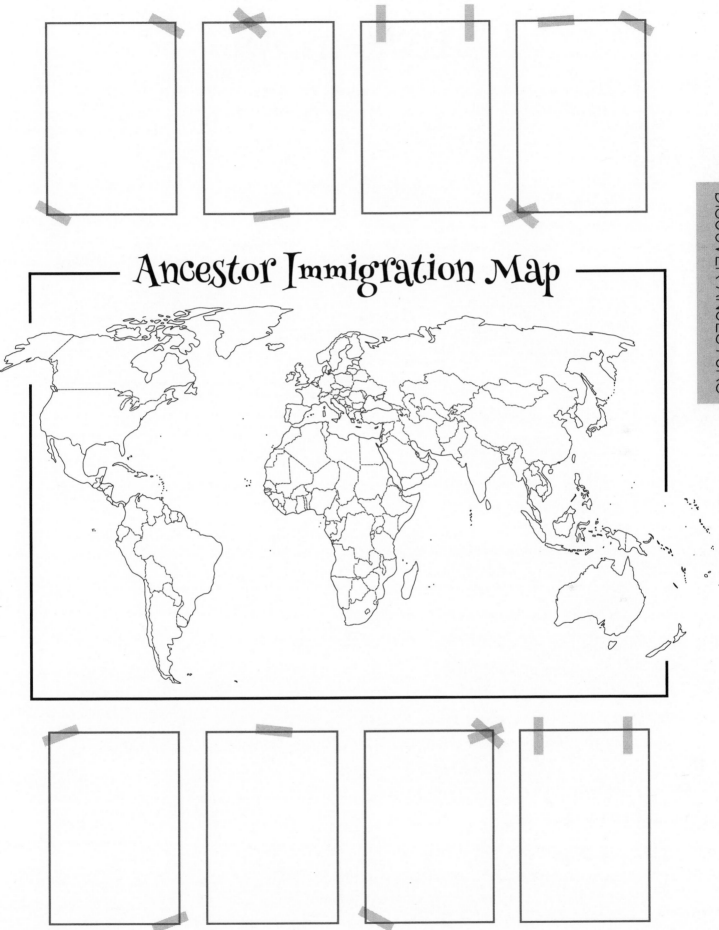

Ancestor Immigration Map

Mission Map

Do you have ancestors who served missions? Perhaps they served while young and single, or maybe they served with a spouse when they were older. Use the blank map on the following page to mark where your ancestors served missions. Draw their faces or write their names in the boxes on the top and bottom, and then draw a line to the place where each ancestor served. Then fill out the chart below.

Materials needed: pen, map on following page

Bonus materials needed: world map poster

	WHO SERVED?	WHERE HE OR SHE SERVED
Coldest mission		
Hottest mission		
Longest mission		
First ancestor to serve		
Left wife and kids behind		
Learned a foreign language		
Served with spouse		
Returned later to live in the mission area		

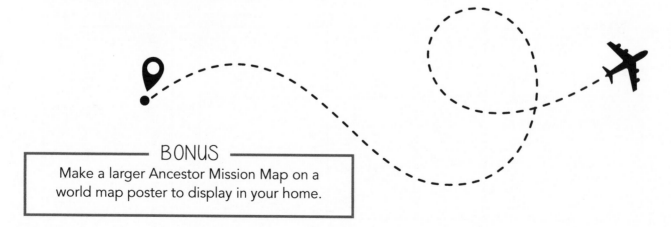

┌─ BONUS ─┐
Make a larger Ancestor Mission Map on a world map poster to display in your home.

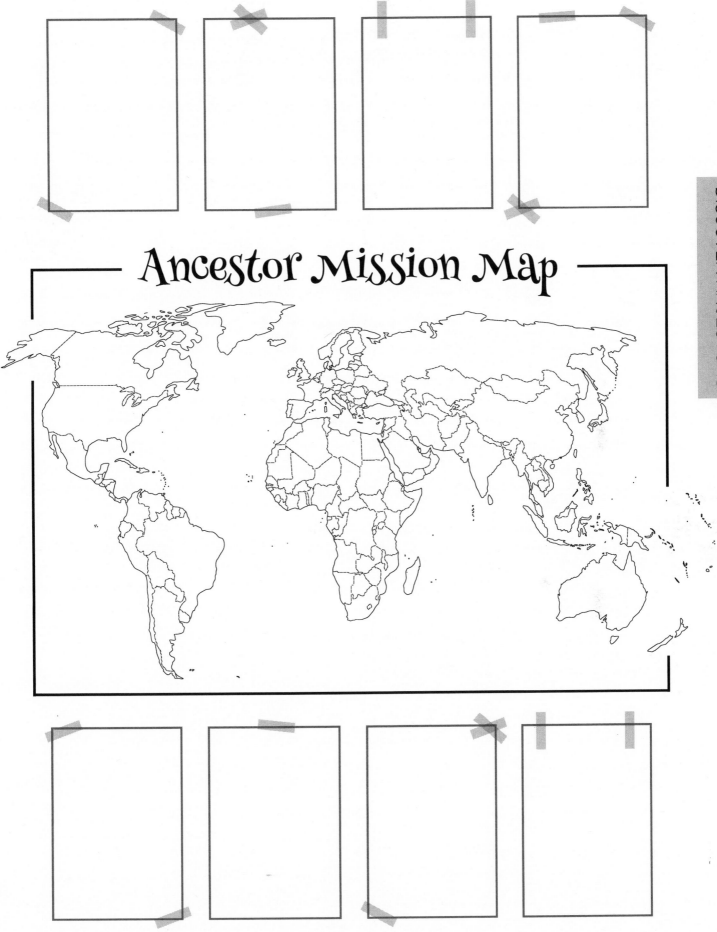

Ancestor Mission Map

Funny Story

Do you know a funny story about an ancestor? Maybe he liked to play jokes on friends, or maybe she was extremely embarrassed by something she did. Discover a funny ancestor story and record it here.

Ancestor's name: _____

Ancestor's birth year: _____

When this story happened: _____

Where this story happened: _____

The funny story:

About My Ancestors

What is another family history topic you can learn about? Use this blank page to write and draw additional information about an ancestor.

_____   _____
Ancestor's name and birth year   Topic

Story: _____
_____
_____
_____
_____
_____

Drawing:

About My Ancestors

What is another family history topic you can learn about? Use this blank page to write and draw additional information about an ancestor.

_____   _____
Ancestor's name and birth year   Topic

Story: _____

_____

_____

_____

_____

_____

Drawing:

Play a Game

Roll the Question Cube

Play this fun question game to learn silly facts about your parents or grandparents. Assemble the cube by cutting it out on the solid lines, folding it on the dotted lines, and gluing or taping the flaps underneath. Then toss it up in the air. When it lands, read aloud the question on top and see what silly things you learn.

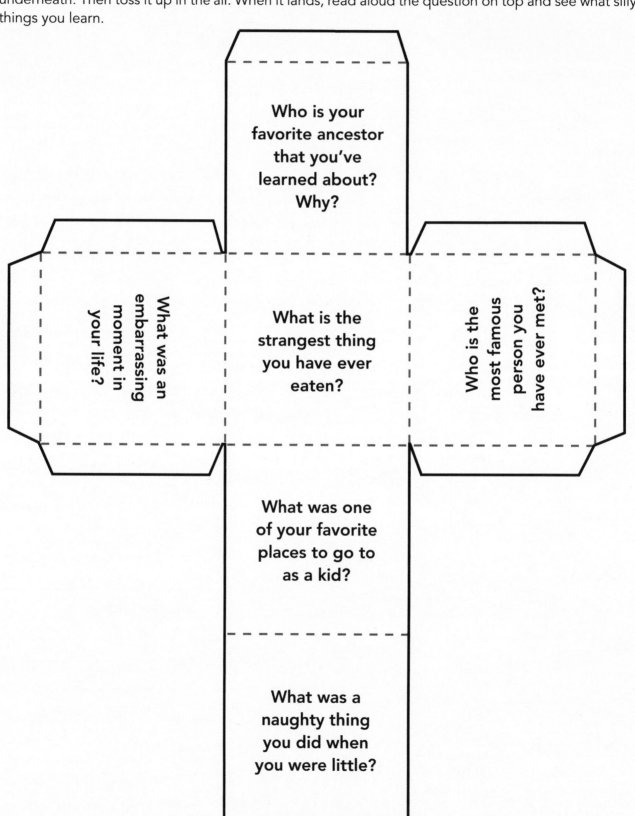

Who is your favorite ancestor that you've learned about? Why?

What was an embarrassing moment in your life?

What is the strangest thing you have ever eaten?

Who is the most famous person you have ever met?

What was one of your favorite places to go to as a kid?

What was a naughty thing you did when you were little?

Play Group Photo I-Spy

Ask your parents to find some photographs of your ancestors in a group of people. It could be a picture of an elementary school class, a family reunion, a community party, a holiday celebration, or a church gathering. Then find your ancestor in the group. Was your ancestor hard or easy to find?

	PLAYER 1 TIME	PLAYER 2 TIME	PLAYER 3 TIME	PLAYER 4 TIME
Photo 1				
Photo 2				
Photo 3				
Photo 4				
Photo 5				
Total time				

--- BONUS ---

Have a timed race between siblings to see how long it takes each of you to find your ancestors' faces in several photographs. Use this table to keep track of times.

Decode Old Handwriting

Have you ever noticed how difficult it is to read handwriting from long ago? Sometimes you wonder whether it is even English you are reading. Find an old handwritten letter, journal entry, or other document that an ancestor wrote. Then complete the activity below.

PLAY A GAME

Copy a few sentences from the old document here, trying to mimic the handwriting.

Now write what it really says in your own handwriting.

BONUS

Play "I Spy" with an old handwritten document. Have someone tell you a word on the paper, and then you try to find it. Then you choose a word, say it, and have the other person find it.

Play Family Name Hangman

If you are familiar with a few names of your ancestors, then you are ready to play. Use those names as the guessing words in the classic paper-and-pencil game of Hangman.

 DIRECTIONS

1. One person is a "host," and another person is a "guesser." The host chooses an ancestor name and makes dashes on the paper to represent each letter of the name. For example, "Loa Tolman" looks like _ _ _   _ _ _ _ _ _.

2. Then the host draws a wooden post, like an upside-down "L," on a piece of paper.

3. The guesser says a letter.

4. If the letter is in the name, the host writes that letter on the corresponding dash.

5. If the letter is not in the name, the host writes that letter on the bottom of the paper (to note that it has already been guessed) and draws one body part on the wooden post.

6. As more correct letters are guessed, the host fills those letters in on the dashes. As more incorrect letters are guessed, the host draws the next body part and writes those letters at the bottom of the paper.

7. If the guesser correctly guesses the ancestor name before the hangman's body is complete, then the guesser wins. If the host completes the hangman's body before the guesser can figure out the ancestor name, then the host wins.

Tip: Before you begin, decide how many guesses (and body parts) you will allow. For example,
10 guesses = head, body line, arm, arm, leg, leg, foot, foot, hand, hand
15 guesses = [same parts as above] PLUS eye, eye, nose, mouth, hair

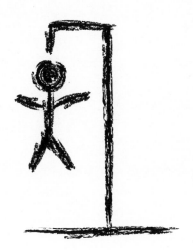

L _ A T _ L _ A N

Reenact Old Photos without Smiling

Look at the faces in some old photographs of ancestors. Do you see any big smiles? Probably not. Is that because people in the 1800s were unhappy? Not at all! There are three theories that could explain why people didn't smile in old photographs. (1) They had to hold completely still for a long time while the old cameras captured the image and a straight face was easier to hold. (2) There were no dentists back then, so everyone had rotten and missing teeth that they wanted to cover. (3) It was desirable to mimic the grand, serious expressions that royalty and presidents had in their paintings. Whatever the reason, a toothy grin was very rare!

Materials needed: an old photograph with serious-looking ancestors, a camera

Bonus materials needed: costumes similar to the ones in the photograph

 DIRECTIONS

1. Find a photograph of your ancestors looking serious and not smiling.
2. With family members or friends, take a picture of you making the same facial expressions and poses as in the photo.
3. Even if you are having a silly time, DON'T SMILE!

BONUS
Can you find or make costumes that resemble the clothes in that old photograph? If so, then dress up and make your reenactment even more accurate.

PLAY A GAME

Act Out Charades

This is a silent acting game that can be extremely silly, especially if the person acting cannot get his or her action correctly guessed and the audience shouts out ridiculous things.

 DIRECTIONS

1. Make about 20 cards with actions from your family history. It could be a job that someone had, an accomplishment they did, a wild adventure they went on, or an embarrassing moment. Use complete sentences on the cards so the people reading them clearly understand what the action is supposed to be, even if they aren't familiar with the story.

2. One person stands in front, randomly chooses a card, reads it in his or her head, and acts out that action silently. No words or noises!

3. The audience tries to guess the action and the ancestor. If they don't know the story, they should at least try to guess what the person is doing. This is where the game can get silly, when people are shouting out very random guesses.

4. The person who guesses the action correctly gets a point. Set a time limit for audience members to guess. If that limit is reached without the correct action guessed, end the round, announce the correct action, and move on to the next round.

5. If you have enough people, you can divide into teams to compete.

Unscramble Your Ancestors

How well can you match your ancestors' faces to their names? This game will test your knowledge.

Materials needed: a copy of a blank family tree (see next page), small copies of the faces of four generations of ancestors

Bonus materials needed: cookie sheet, small magnets, glue

 DIRECTIONS

1. Fill out four generations of your ancestors' names on the blank family tree.

2. Cut out copies of your ancestors' faces to match the size of the rectangles on the family tree.

3. Mix up the cut out faces so they are out of order and then place the cut out faces on the corresponding ancestor name on the family tree.

PLAY A GAME

How many could you correctly match by yourself? _____

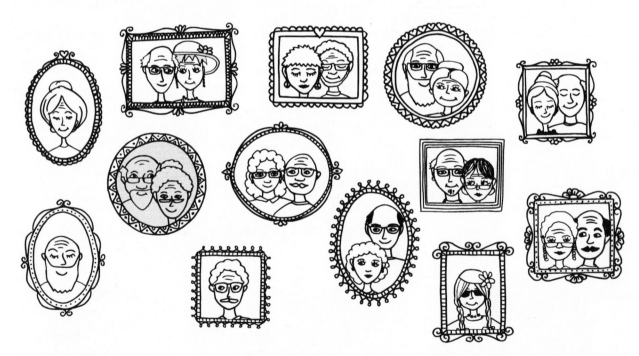

BONUS

To make this a more permanent game or display, you can glue the family tree paper to a small cookie sheet and glue the face pieces onto magnets. Store the face magnets on the edge of the cookie sheet, and you can play the game whenever you want. See how many matches you can do by yourself, and try to improve each week. Or you can hang the cookie sheet on your wall and display the faces in the correct places.

PLACE PICTURES HERE TO BEGIN

PLACE PICTURES HERE TO BEGIN

Make a Jigsaw Puzzle

Do you enjoy putting together jigsaw puzzles? If you do, then you may like making your own puzzle! Here's how.

Materials needed: copy of an ancestor's picture, glue, thin cardboard, and scissors

 DIRECTIONS

1. Get a copy of an ancestor's photograph that you love.
2. Glue that picture onto a thin piece of cardboard. (Cereal boxes work really well.)
3. Draw jigsaw puzzle piece lines on the picture. (See image below for typical puzzle piece shapes.)
4. Cut out the pieces on the lines you drew.
5. Assemble the puzzle.

Example of typical puzzle piece shapes

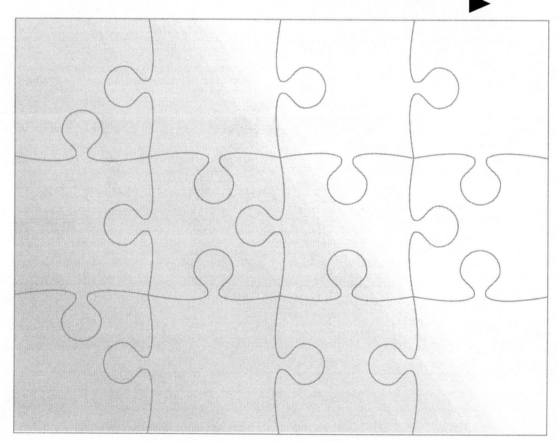

— BONUS —
Time your parents and siblings to see who can complete the puzzle the fastest.

Play an Ancestor Memory Game

Have you ever played a game of memory, where you turn over cards to see if the images underneath match? It's a fun game. Try making your own memory game cards with images you would like to remember, like the faces of your ancestors!

Materials needed: copies of your ancestors' faces printed or mounted on cardstock

 DIRECTIONS

1. Have an adult help you copy and mount TWO SETS of many of your ancestors' faces on cardstock.
2. Cut them into equally sized cards.
3. Shuffle the cards and place them face down in a grid on the table.
4. One person flips over two cards. If the cards do not match, flip them facing down again and move on to step 5. If the cards match, that person keeps those cards in a "Correct Match" pile in front of him or her and then gets an additional turn to flip over two new cards.
5. The other person begins his or her turn by repeating step 4.
6. After all the cards have been matched and put in the "Correct Match" piles, the game is over. The person with the most matches wins.

BONUS

The more cards there are in the game, the more challenging it is. Keep adding more sets of ancestors' faces to the deck and see if you can still remember where matches are.

Play Ancestor BINGO

BINGO can be a great way to become familiar with ancestors' names and faces while having fun. This is also a great way to enjoy some candy!

Materials needed: 24 photos of ancestors, computer, printer, cardstock, scissors, candy pieces

 DIRECTIONS

1. On a computer document or chart program, create a grid with 24 ancestor photographs. You can put a picture of yourself in the middle square for a "free" space.
2. Print several copies, each one with the faces scrambled around so each game card is different.
3. Print an additional sheet. Cut each face out of that sheet and put the 24 faces in a basket or bag.
4. Take turns pulling out one face from the "draw" basket. All players put a piece of candy on that ancestor's face on their own sheets.
5. The first person to have five candies in a row, in a column, or on a diagonal wins the game.

Test Your Timeline Knowledge

The lives of your ancestors were filled with triumphal, tragic, exciting, and scary events that changed their personalities and lives. Learn about eight events in an ancestor's life. Write the events in the boxes below. Then copy the information onto craft sticks. Scramble the order of the events. Then see if you can put the events back in the correct order.

Materials needed: knowledge of eight events in an ancestor's life, paper, scissors, craft sticks

Write the events here.

Host a Family History Quiz Show

Test your family's knowledge of your ancestors and their stories in a fun, competitive way. This is a perfect activity for a big family gathering.

Materials needed: 20 questions and answers about your ancestors, notecards, tape, markers

 DIRECTIONS

1. Prepare 20 questions about your ancestors' names, jobs, talents, marriages, children, events, accomplishments, locations, service, accidents, etc. Including funny stories is an absolute must. You can group the questions into categories if you want to.

2. Write each question on a notecard and keep the answers on a separate answer key. Tape the question notecards to a large board or wall. Then tape a blank notecard over each question to cover it. Write point values on each of those blank cards.

3. Split the participants into teams and have them make team names.

4. One person from the first team chooses a question to be read aloud. Once the question is read, any team can race to answer it first. The team that answers it correctly first gets the points. Or, to be a little less competitive, all teams who get the correct answer can get the points.

5. The team that has the most points at the end of all the questions wins.

Play "I'm Thinking of an Ancestor"

This is a quick and easy game to play at the dinner table, in the car, or while waiting for a doctor's appointment. It requires no preparation and no supplies.

 DIRECTIONS

1. One person thinks of an ancestor. He says aloud, "I'm thinking of an ancestor who . . ." and says a fact about that ancestor. Depending on the age of those who are listening, he can give obvious clues or challenging clues.

2. The people who are listening guess which ancestor the person is talking about.

3. The person giving clues keeps giving clues until the correct ancestor has been guessed.

Guess What Is on Your Forehead

This is a silly game that can leave you and the people you play with laughing loudly, confused completely, or a funny mix of both.

Materials needed: notecards, markers, masking tape

 DIRECTIONS

1. Have the participants write words relating to their ancestors on notecards. They can write names, traditions, locations, jokes, food, countries, etc. Let them decide.

2. Shuffle the cards and have each participant pick one without looking at it.

3. Help the participants tape their chosen card, facing out, to their forehead.

4. All at the same time, the participants wander around the room and ask "yes or no" questions, such as, "Am I a person?" "Am I something from a long time ago?" "Am I something silly?" "Have I seen this thing ever?" When you answer others' questions, only answer with a "yes" or a "no"! Describing the words on the card is cheating!

5. Once a person correctly guesses the word on their forehead, they take the card off and continue wandering around answering others' questions until everyone has correctly guessed the word on their forehead.

Solve Family History Sudoku

For children under age 8

➡ DIRECTIONS ⬅

Fill in the full grid so that every row, column, and mini-grid contains one of each symbol. (When you look across each row, each symbol should appear only once. As you look down each column, each symbol should appear only once. As you look in a mini-grid of four that is designated by a bold line, each symbol should appear only once.) Use a pencil, because you may need to erase your pictures as you are solving the puzzle.

♡ **Heart**—What ancestor do you love the most?

😆 **Smile**—What ancestor makes you smile?

🌲 **Tree**—How are your ancestors like strong tree roots?

⭐ **Star**—Which ancestor would you like to meet?

Solve Family History Sudoku

For children age 8 and older

DIRECTIONS

Complete the puzzle. Each row, each column, and each small square group of nine must only have one heart, magnifying glass, camera, smile, tree, temple, check mark, star, and book in it.

Heart symbol—Which ancestor do you love hearing about?

Magnifying Glass symbol—What objects have you seen that have helped you learn about your ancestors?

Camera symbol—What are the most interesting pictures you have seen of your ancestors?

Smile symbol—Which ancestors make you smile?

Tree symbol—Why is a tree a common symbol of family history?

Globe symbol—What countries are your ancestors from?

Check Mark symbol—Do you know the names of all your great-grandparents?

Star symbol—Which ancestor in the past would you like to meet?

Book symbol—Flip through this book and find the next activity you would like to do.

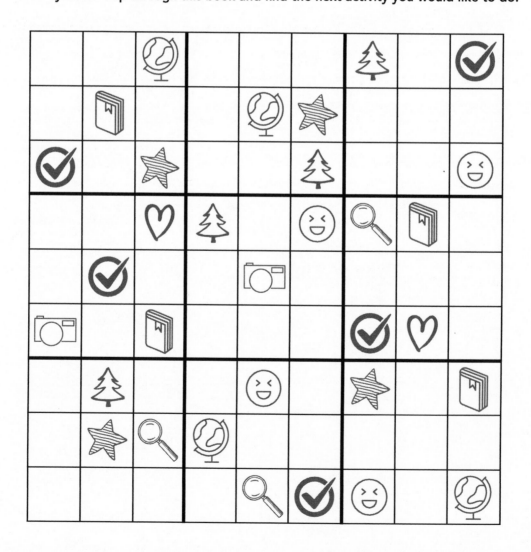

PLAY A GAME

Fill Out the Family Titles Crossword Puzzle

There are so many titles for all the people in your family—mom, nephew, grandmother, cousin, and so on. If you know them all, you can feel confident when you talk about the people in your family and when you attend family reunions. Test your knowledge of family titles with this crossword puzzle.

ACROSS

1. Your parent's sister
5. Your parent's brother
7. Your aunt and uncle's child
9. Your female parent
11. Your parent's father
12. Your sibling's son
13. Your male sibling

DOWN

2. Your sibling's daughter
3. Your female child
4. Your male child
6. Your male parent
8. Your parent's mother
10. Your female sibling

--- BONUS ---

What are the given names of all these people in your family?
Write them next to their titles on the lists above.

Find the Family History Topics

Find these words that describe various family history topics you can learn about. All these neat topics have individual worksheets in the previous section that you can fill out for your ancestors. Which topics are you interested in learning about?

PLAY A GAME

```
I  J  Z  R  D  A  I  A  Y  G  G  D  K  E  F  Z  C  T  B  W
N  G  M  U  S  I  C  P  C  S  U  O  C  L  N  A  F  G  U  S
Y  D  A  F  K  E  O  G  T  C  X  Q  L  H  S  B  M  F  M  H
Q  F  W  R  K  J  L  E  S  H  C  N  P  U  O  T  W  I  A  Y
U  O  J  Y  D  T  D  I  Y  O  I  G  E  Z  F  R  H  X  L  D
B  G  E  R  M  E  L  X  J  O  M  H  T  V  U  D  E  V  T  Y
I  Z  W  D  J  O  N  B  C  L  M  A  S  Q  N  X  P  S  N  Y
R  C  V  W  J  N  T  L  F  B  I  N  I  A  N  S  F  F  N  J
T  D  N  K  O  O  F  T  I  O  G  D  I  Y  Y  U  M  O  R  B
H  H  N  P  B  U  K  Y  O  X  R  W  W  A  R  R  P  O  O  R
P  I  R  P  W  V  P  D  I  D  A  R  W  E  C  V  L  D  Y  K
L  S  Q  O  E  H  G  M  N  A  N  I  G  F  H  I  S  H  Y  U
A  T  X  E  D  A  T  I  J  C  T  T  X  F  I  V  P  E  W  E
C  O  X  M  D  N  F  S  U  E  C  I  K  E  L  O  O  I  M  B
E  R  Z  R  I  D  R  S  R  J  W  N  H  C  D  R  R  R  U  J
B  Y  K  S  N  M  R  I  Y  U  K  G  H  T  H  J  T  L  L  E
S  X  H  N  G  A  C  O  N  V  E  R  T  F  O  D  S  O  R  M
R  L  R  T  D  D  L  N  X  B  C  A  W  T  O  Q  M  O  K  R
I  A  H  W  E  E  R  J  O  U  R  N  A  L  D  D  U  M  V  O
F  J  E  T  G  Z  A  Y  G  D  W  X  R  U  S  A  D  K  K  F
```

WORD LIST

BIRTHPLACE	FOOD	HISTORY	MISSION	SCHOOL
CHILDHOOD	FUNNY	IMMIGRANT	MOTTO	SPORTS
CHORES	GARDEN	INJURY	MUSIC	SURVIVOR
CONVERT	HANDMADE	JOB	PETS	WAR
EFFECT	HANDWRITING	JOURNAL	POEM	WEDDING
FAMILY	HEIRLOOM			

Create Your Own Word Search or Crossword Puzzle

There are free word search and crossword puzzle generators online. Find a good one with the help of a parent and decide what words you will use. Then insert the words into the program online, generate a word search, print it, and give it to someone to solve.

Words I want to include:

Play "Decisions Determine Destiny"

Even though your children or grandchildren have not even been born yet, the decisions you make in the next ten years and beyond will greatly affect them. Play a stacking block game that requires you to pull out a block from the tower and place it on top.

 DIRECTIONS

1. When you pull a block out and the tower is still steady, say a choice you can make that will strengthen your future family.

2. When you pull a block out that makes the tower wobbly, say a choice you can make that will hurt your future family.

3. You can also share decisions ancestors made that affected you for good or for ill.

4. When the tower finally collapses, rebuild it to show that families are resilient and can rebuild after hard times.

PLAY A GAME

Make a Craft

Illustrate Your Own Storybook

Have you ever wanted to be an author or an illustrator—or maybe both? Here is your chance. Gather your favorite family history stories. Get some blank paper. Write text for the story on the bottom and create your own illustration on the top. Divide the story into as many or as few pages as you want. Insert your pages into plastic sheet protectors and put them into a three-ring binder. Use the boxes and lines below to draft your first story.

Materials needed: stories, paper, markers, plastic sleeves, binder

Make an Important Family Date Calendar

We usually use calendars to remember important dates and events that will happen in the future, but we can also use calendars to remember special events that have happened in the past. Fill out this chart with your ancestors' birthdays, baptism days, immigration days, wedding days, death days, victory days, etc., that you want to remember each month.

Materials needed: your current calendar, a blank calendar, or this page

January _____   July _____

_____   _____

_____   _____

_____   _____

February _____   August _____

_____   _____

_____   _____

_____   _____

March _____   September _____

_____   _____

_____   _____

_____   _____

April _____   October _____

_____   _____

_____   _____

_____   _____

May _____   November _____

_____   _____

_____   _____

_____   _____

June _____   December _____

_____   _____

_____   _____

_____   _____

BONUS

Use an online calendar-making program to create a special ancestor calendar. Insert photographs of ancestors on the top pages, and fill in special events in the date squares.

Sew a "Quilt of Many Generations"

The first thing we touch when we wake up and the last thing we touch when we go to sleep is a blanket. If you have a blanket that reminds you of your ancestors, thinking of them can be the first and last thing you do each day.

Materials needed: blanket-making supplies

Select which blanket-making method will be best for you:

1. Ask your parents, grandparents, and great-grandparents for old fabrics they collected or old pieces of clothing that they don't mind being cut up. Sew those fabrics together to make a Quilt of Many Generations.

2. Print your favorite ancestors' photographs on photo transfer paper (available at craft stores). Follow the directions to print, cut, and iron on the paper so that the image is transferred to white fabric. Then sew the fabric pieces together to make an Ancestor Photo Blanket.

3. Ask your family members who can quilt to make a section of a quilt for you. Then sew them all together to make a family quilt.

4. Find an online photo gift website that makes the blanket for you. All you need to do is upload the photographs and select the style. The company makes the blanket and sends it to you.

Design a Family Shirt

The shirts you wear send a message to other people about you. Let your friends know the love you feel for your family by designing and making a family shirt. Design your shirt below first. Then use fabric markers, puffy paints, vinyl, or iron-on paper on a blank T-shirt to make a family shirt that you can wear with pride.

Materials needed: a shirt, iron-on transfers, or vinyl cut-outs or cloth markers

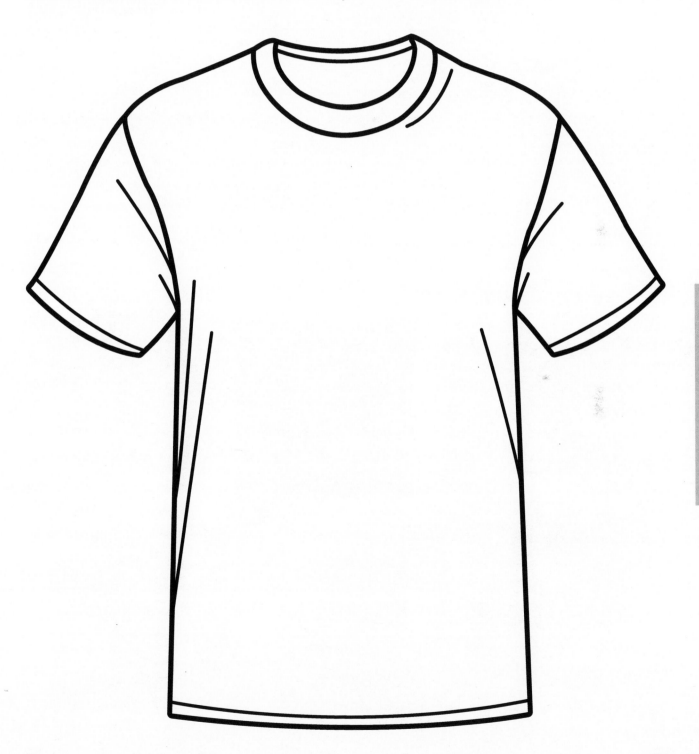

Trace a Shadow Silhouette

If your ancestors didn't have access to a camera or a set of fancy paints and an artist, they had few options to document how they looked. But one way they could document their faces was by making a shadow silhouette. You can make one of yourself and anyone else you want to. Hang your silhouette on the wall next to some ancestors' black and white photographs.

Materials needed: white paper, black paper, tape, pencil, scissors, flashlight or lamp

 DIRECTIONS

1. Tape a white piece of paper to a wall.
2. Sit down on a chair, sideways, near the paper on the wall.
3. Shine a light behind your head so you cast a shadow of the side of your face on the wall. Adjust the light until your shadow is crisp.
4. Have a friend or family member trace your face's shadow on the white paper.
5. Cut out the silhouette on the white paper, and then trace it onto black paper. (This extra step is important, because it is difficult to trace a shadow directly onto black paper.)
6. Cut out the silhouette on the black paper and glue it onto white or colored paper. Write your name underneath and frame it on the wall.

Hang Labeled Pictures in Your Room

Displaying a photo of a strong ancestor in your room can have a powerful effect on your attitude, mood, and perspective. For example, if you are sad about having to share your room, your clothes, and your toys, thinking of your ancestor who shared a room with eight siblings, had no toys, and had only one outfit may help you feel better about your own situation. Choose an ancestor who gives you perspective and strength. Copy a picture of him or her and frame it. With a permanent marker, write on the glass or the frame what you want to remember and feel.

Materials needed: photograph, frame, permanent marker

Which ancestor do I want to remember when my life gets tough?

_____

What do I want to remember when I see this picture?

_____

_____

_____

_____

BE GRATEFUL FOR WHAT YOU HAVE

Colorize a Black-and-White Photo

Have you ever noticed that all old photographs are black and white? The world was colorful, but cameras couldn't capture it. Colorizing old photographs is a technique to make the world of the past more real to us. Photocopy an ancestor photograph on a light setting, so that there is minimal black ink. Then use colored pencils or crayons to color the face, clothing, and background.

Materials needed: a light copy of an ancestor's photograph, colored pencils

─── BONUS ───
Make a colorful frame out of craft sticks to display your colorized photo in. Glue four (or more) craft sticks together and decorate them with a variety of craft supplies (glitter, sequins, pom-poms, puffy paint, yarn, stickers, beads, buttons, etc.). Hang it in your room, in your locker at school, on your car rearview mirror, on your Christmas tree, on your fridge, or on your dresser.

Create Your Own Coloring Book

Transform a few old photographs into a coloring book just for you.

Materials needed: photographs of your ancestors, blank paper, thick black pen, tape, window

 DIRECTIONS

1. Get several photographs of one of your ancestors. Try to have a variety of images, such as a face, a house, some hobbies, a baby picture, or an adult picture.

2. Tape the photograph to a sunny window.

3. Tape a blank paper over that photo on the window.

4. Look through the blank paper to the photograph and see the image. Trace a very simple outline of that image onto your blank paper.

5. Remove the blank paper, and you will now have a simple outline that you can color.

6. Make several tracings of photographs you like and staple them together to make a coloring book.

Set Up a Photo Booth

It's fun to set up a photo booth and take pictures of you and your family holding props. Make a backdrop by hanging a plain sheet or by decorating a wall in your house like the background of old photographs. Then make props that represent the clothing, interests, talents, or traits of your ancestors.

Materials needed: cardstock, printer or markers, unsharpened pencils or grilling skewers, glue, hot glue, or strong tape

 DIRECTIONS

1. Set up a backdrop to have behind you in all the pictures.
2. Print out various props on cardstock, or simply draw them on cardstock.
3. Cut the props out.
4. Glue the props with a hot glue gun (or tape) to the tops of long pencils or grill skewers.
5. Hold the props up to your face, head, or chest as someone takes your picture.

IDEAS FOR PROPS

Mustaches and beards	Fancy hats, top hats, feather hats
Hats particular to a profession	Hair with a giant perm, or curls on the forehead
Glasses or monocles	Word bubbles with ancestors' expressions
Lips making silly expressions	Pocket watch
Medals from military or sports	Brooches and necklaces
Neckties or bowties	Scarves
Handheld fans	Tools

MAKE A CRAFT

Design a Family Crest

Long ago, kings granted to families crests that had symbols of skill and accomplishment. Families displayed their crests with pride, and knights even had their family's crest on the front of their shields. They went to battle with their family crest protecting them. Design a coat of arms for your family. What about your family are you proud of? What symbols show the skills and accomplishments of your family, past and present? Use this blank family crest, or make a larger one of your own to display in your home.

Bonus materials needed: cardboard or a fake plastic shield, markers

• MY COAT OF ARMS •

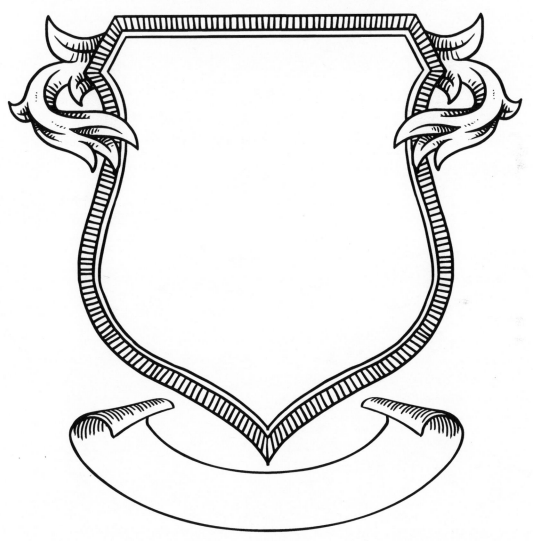

── BONUS ──
Make a battle shield with your family crest on it. Glue your design to a piece of sturdy cardboard. Cut out the crest in the shape of a shield. Then cut out an additional piece of cardboard to glue to the back and use as a handle.

Make a Charm Bracelet

Charm bracelets can be pretty reminders of our ancestors. Below are some ideas of how you can make your own.

Materials needed: various supplies to make charm bracelets

1. Use yarn and uncooked pasta to make a bracelet. Cut out small charms from cardboard in various shapes. Glue small copies of ancestors' faces on them. Thread the yarn through the ripples in the middle of the cardboard.

2. Go to a craft store and buy bracelet-making supplies. Find beads that you like, and look through the charms to find ones that represent the interests, talents, traits, or facts about your ancestors.

3. Make your own beads out of polymer clay. You can make simple spheres, colorful cubes, or even make special shapes that have to do with your ancestors, such as the animals they liked, the sports they played, or the places they lived. Bake the beads in your oven before threading them together.

4. Make paper beads by rolling skinny triangular strips of paper around a toothpick. Apply glue to the tip of each triangle before finishing rolling. Once it's dry, coat the bead in a craft sealer.

5. Buy a set of transparent clear domed glass cabochon covers for alloy photo pendant making. Insert tiny photos of ancestors' faces between the metal backing and the domed glass topping to make beautiful pendants of your family. Add these to a bracelet with beads.

6. Find a charm-bracelet-making website and order exactly what you want.

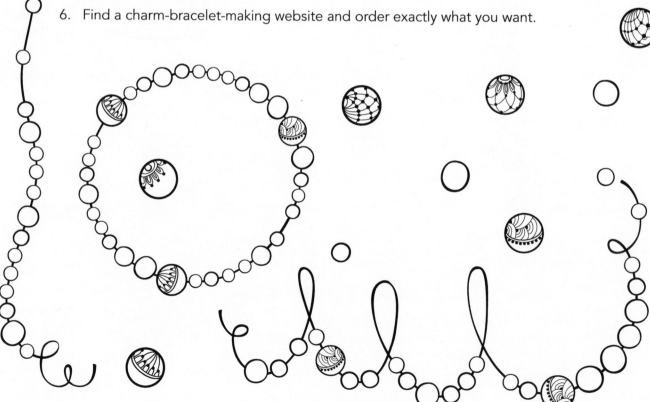

Make a Locket

Lockets are beautiful necklaces with two halves that hinge open to reveal tiny photographs inside. Make your own locket to remember your ancestors. Use a template below to draw or cut out a locket from lightweight cardboard. Fold it in half. Glue a copy of an ancestor's picture inside the locket. Decorate the outside. Thread yarn through the hole and tie the locket around your neck.

Materials needed: thin cardboard, copy of photograph, yarn, other decorating supplies

BONUS
Find a real locket at the store or online. Insert your ancestor's photograph into the real locket and wear it as jewelry.

Make Dog Tags

"Dog tags" are the identification tags that soldiers wear on a chain around their necks to help identify their bodies if wounded or killed in combat. These have been used since World War I. If you have an ancestor who fought in any war since then, they probably wore dog tags. Make a copy of the ones they wore by following these directions.

Materials needed: aluminum foil, cardboard, glue, yarn or necklace chain

 DIRECTIONS

Trace and cut out these templates. Then trace the shapes onto thin cardboard. Cut out the cardboard, including the hole for the yarn or chain. Carefully wrap and glue aluminum foil around the cardboard, keeping the foil on the front as smooth as possible. Use a ballpoint pen to etch the information onto the foil. (The two tags should be identical, but you can make them different if you choose.) Thread yarn or a ball chain through the hole. Tie the ends together and put the dog tag around your neck.

ACTUAL INFO ON ID TAGS	OTHER INFO YOU MAY INCLUDE
Name	**Military rank**
Social Security #	**Hometown**
Blood Type	**Place where he or she fought**
Religion	**War he or she fought in**
	Dates of service

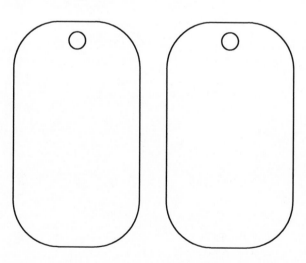

BONUS
Find a company online or a booth inside a department store that makes real dog tags. Insert the words you want on it, order it, and they will send it to you.

Make a Guardian Angel Display

A wise spiritual leader once said this about our deceased ancestors: "Those who have been faithful, who have gone beyond . . . can see us better than we can see them . . . they know us better than we know them. . . . We live in their presence, they see us, they are solicitous for our welfare, they love us now more than ever. For now they see the dangers that beset us; . . . their love for us and their desire for our well-being must be greater than that which we feel for ourselves."[1]

Use the frame template below, or put a copy of a photo of a deceased ancestor in a frame that you make or buy. Then glue some white feathers around it to remind you of your guardian angel.

Materials needed: copy of an ancestor's photo, store-bought or homemade frame, glue, real or fake white feathers

1. Joseph F. Smith, in Conference Report, Apr. 1916, as quoted by Richard G. Scott, "How to Obtain Revelation and Inspiration in Your Personal Life," *Ensign*, May 2012.

Produce a Puppet Show

Put on a puppet show highlighting a story from an ancestor's life. It could be a silly story, a story of courage, or anything else. You can use puppets you already have, or you can make your own puppets with decorated socks, sewn felt, or craft sticks with ancestor's photos glued on them. Sit behind a cloth-covered table, and hold your puppets above the table so your audience can see the puppets but not you.

Materials needed: puppets or puppet-making supplies

Ancestor's name: _____

Story I will act out: _____

_____

_____

_____

Puppets I need to make: _____

_____

Audience: _____

_____

Paint Family Rocks

In some places, people paint rocks with all sorts of designs and then hide them around town for others to find. Have you ever found a painted rock? Try making your own. Find and clean a flat, oval rock. Paint on it an ancestor's face, a country's flag, a family motto, or another symbol of your family. Use the oval below to practice drawing what you will put on your rock.

Materials needed: flat river rock, acrylic paint pens or acrylic paints and brush

be creative

I will paint this on a rock:

Make a Flipbook

You can bring an ancestor's story to life by making a flipbook. A flipbook is a book of illustrations that seem to move as you flip through it.

Materials needed: a light-colored sticky note pad, pen

 DIRECTIONS

1. Choose a brief ancestor story to animate. Write a title and draw a cover on the top sticky note.

2. On the LAST sticky note, draw a simple drawing.

3. Flip to the second-to-last note, and see your first drawing appear through that note. Use that as a reference as you draw your next illustration, which should be similar to the first but slightly different as your ancestor moves.

4. Continue drawing a new illustration on each sticky note, using the one underneath as a reference.

5. After you've drawn on each sticky note, put your thumb on the side of the book and release the pages down gradually so they flip past. It will seem like your drawing is coming to life.

Decorate Paper Doll Chains

Use the templates on the next two pages to make paper doll chains of your family. Put a blank paper over these templates and trace the body images. Accordion-fold your paper back and forth on the dotted lines. Cut out the lines that you traced. When you cut out the top image, all the people beneath are cut out too. Unfold the chain and decorate the people. You can use crayons, or you can glue real photographs of family members' faces on the heads and use pieces of real fabric and buttons for clothing.

Materials needed: paper, scissors, decorating supplies

Decorate a Boy Paper Doll Chain

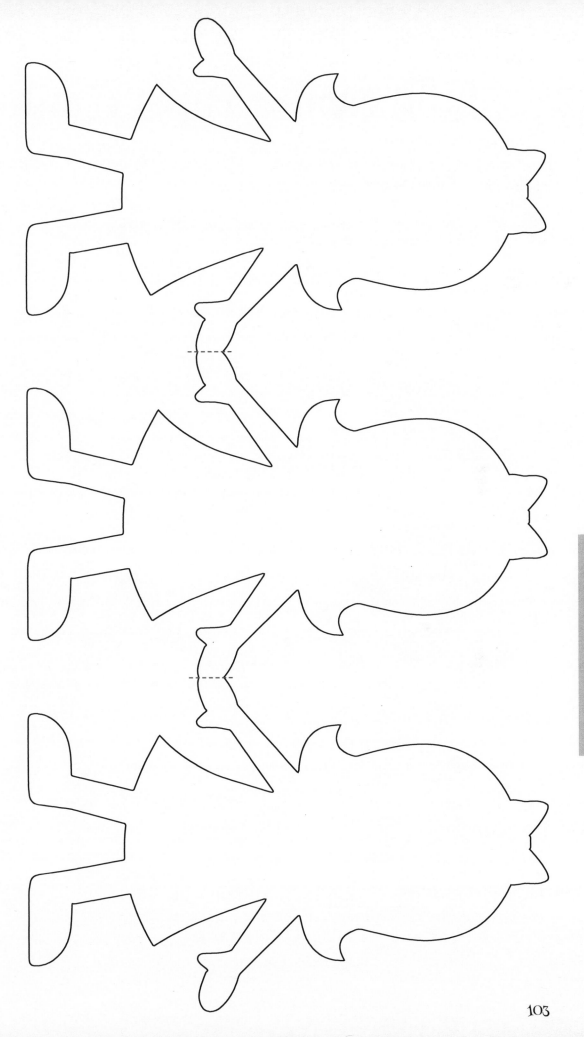

Decorate a Girl Paper Doll Chain

Link Family Paper Chains

You are linked to all of your ancestors for hundreds and thousands of years before you. You are all like links in a chain, connected and strong. Make a paper chain of ancestors that you can hang on your curtain rod, on an indoor tree, or above your bed.

Materials needed: strips of colored paper, scissors, pictures of your ancestors' faces (optional)

 DIRECTIONS

1. Cut out many strips of colored paper about 1 inch wide and 8 inches long, like the sample below.

2. On each strip, write a different ancestor's name. To make the chain longer, include all your siblings, cousins, aunts, uncles, etc. If you want to, glue a picture of that relative's face to the strip of paper.

3. When the strips are finished, hold the two sides of one strip together and staple or tape them to make a loop.

4. Insert a second strip into the loop you just made and tape or glue those ends together. Repeat these steps until you have linked together all the strips into a chain.

SAMPLE PAPER STRIP SIZE

MAKE A CRAFT

Make a Family Christmas Tree

We celebrate Jesus Christ at Christmas. Because of Him, our families can feel more joy in this life and can live together forever in the next life. So this Christmas, decorate your tree with family history ornaments. Here are some ideas:

- Buy several tiny frames and glue a loop of string on the top for hanging.
- Make your own frames with craft sticks. Decorate them with glitter, puffy paint, stickers, buttons, pom-poms, beads, etc.
- Hang a paper chain on the tree with your ancestors' names (see previous activity).
- Buy colorful round ornaments and use a decoupage glue to attach copies of old photographs to the ornaments, or just write names on them.
- Cut out a variety of shapes (heart, star, luggage tag, tree, circle, rectangle, sun) and glue your ancestors' pictures on them. Loop a piece of yarn through a hole in the top.

Materials needed: various ornament making supplies

Make Art with Old Silverware

There was a period of time when couples enjoyed purchasing a fancy set of silverware to eat with on special occasions. They treasured this set of spoons, forks, and knives and spent hours polishing them to keep them shiny. But that silverware set they loved is probably sitting in a closet getting dusty and tarnished. Pull it out and make art with the utensils to help you remember that ancestor.

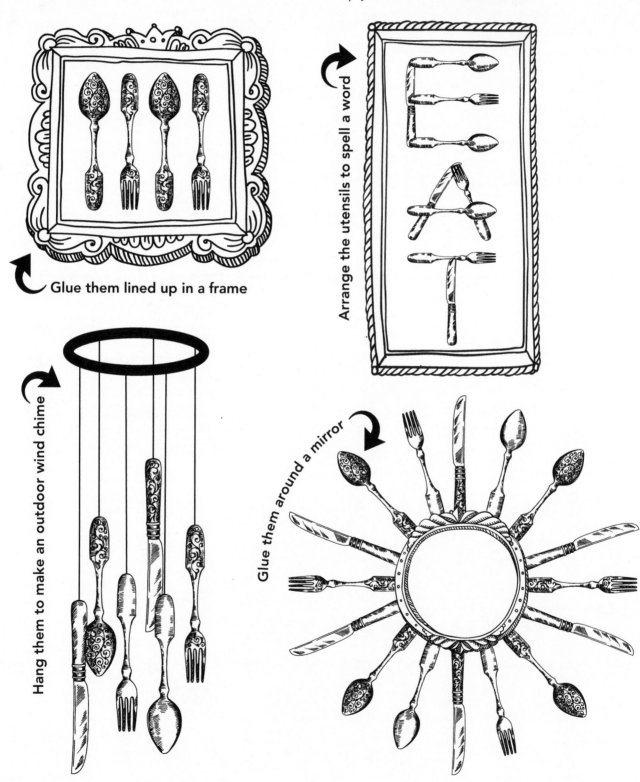

Glue them lined up in a frame

Arrange the utensils to spell a word

Hang them to make an outdoor wind chime

Glue them around a mirror

106

See How Much You Know Now

Now that you have done a lot of activities about your ancestors, see how many of their names you can write on this blank tree. We're hoping that you can fill out more names now than you could in the first tree at the beginning of this book!

MY FOUR-GENERATION FAMILY TREE

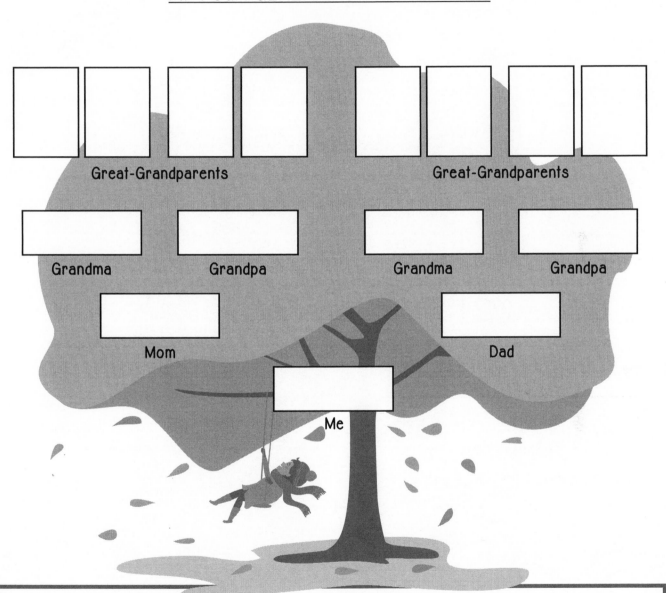

Great-Grandparents

Great-Grandparents

Grandma

Grandpa

Grandma

Grandpa

Mom

Dad

Me

How many of your ancestors' names did you know by yourself? _____

How many of your ancestors' names did your parents help you fill in? _____

How many of your ancestors' names did you and your parents have to look up? _____

Total ancestors in four-generation family tree: _____

BONUS: Can you write in at the top of the tree other distant ancestors' names that you know?

MAKE A CRAFT

107

About the Authors

CHARLOTTE AND JONAH first met while working on family history in their university library. Since then, they have written extensively about their own ancestors, presented at various family history conferences, and conducted research about youth and their family stories. One of their main goals in life is to make family history a fun and meaningful pastime for young people. Charlotte and Jonah also enjoy playing music, goofing around with their six children, raising chickens, and running their wholesale bakery in Vancouver, Washington.

SHARE YOUR EXPERIENCES AND YOUR NEW IDEAS WITH US!

www.TurningLittleHearts.com